Mysteries Make You Think

DD
There is a rapidly growing public interest in farm animal welfare and some demand for organically produced food.
G
S
H
The roots of trees and bushes help support rabbit burrows.
I
T
U

Theory INTO Practice

Mysteries Make You Think

DAVID LEAT
and
ADAM NICHOLS

PROFESSIONAL DEVELOPMENT FOR GEOGRAPHY TEACHERS
Series editors: Mary Biddulph and Graham Butt

Acknowledgements

Students and teachers of Blyth Tynedale High School, Northumberland; Heaton Manor School, Newcastle upon Tyne; and Framwellgate Moor Comprehensive School, Durham.

The authors

Dr D.J.K. Leat is Senior Lecturer, Department of Education, University of Newcastle upon Tyne, St Thomas Street, Newcastle upon Tyne NE1 3RU and Mr T.A.H. Nichols is a key stage 3 National Strategy Foundations Subjects Consultant for the City of Sunderland LEA, formerly a Lecturer in Education at the University of Durham.

The series editors

Dr Mary Biddulph is Lecturer in Geography Education in the School of Education, University of Nottingham and Dr Graham Butt is Senior Lecturer in Geographical Education in the School of Education, University of Birmingham.

ISBN 1 899085 70 X
First published 1999, revised 2003
Impression number 10 9 8 7 6 5 4 3 2 1
Year 2007, 2006, 2005, 2004

Published by the Geographical Association, 160 Solly Street, Sheffield S1 4BF. The Geographical Association is a registered charity: no 313129.

The Publications Officer of the GA would be happy to hear from other potential authors who have ideas for geography books. You may contact the Officer via the GA at the address above. The views expressed in this publication are those of the authors and do not necessarily represent those of the Geographical Association.

Designed by Ledgard Jepson Limited
Printed and bound in China, through Colorcraft Ltd, Hong Kong

Contents

Editors' preface

Theory into Practice is dedicated to improving both teaching and learning in geography. The over-riding element in the series is direct communication with the classroom practitioner about current research in geographical education and how this relates to classroom practice. Geography teachers from across the professional spectrum will be able to access research findings on particular issues which they can then relate to their own particular context.

How to use this series

This series also has a number of other concerns. First, we seek to achieve the further professional development of geography teachers and their departments. Second, each book is intended to support teachers' thinking about key aspects of teaching and learning in geography and encourages them to reconsider these in the light of research findings. Third, we hope to reinvigorate the debate about how to teach geography and to give teachers the support and encouragement to revisit essential questions, such as:.

- Why am I teaching this topic?
- Why am I teaching it in this way?
- Is there a more enjoyable/challenging/interesting/successful way to teach this?
- What are the students learning?
- How are they learning?
- Why are they learning?

This list is by no means exhaustive and there are many other key questions which geography teachers can and should ask. However, the ideas discussed and issues raised in this series provide a framework for thinking about practice. Fourth, each book should offer teachers of geography a vehicle within which they can improve the quality of teaching and learning in their subject; and an opportunity to arm themselves with the new understandings about geography and geographical education. With this information teachers can challenge current assumptions about the nature of the subject in schools. The intended outcome is to support geography teachers in becoming part of the teaching and learning debate. Finally, the series aims to make classroom practitioners feel better informed about their own practice through consideration of, and reflection upon, the research into what they do best - teach geography.

Mary Biddulph and Graham Butt
July 1999

Introduction

The *Thinking Through Geography* (TTG) group, which has been instrumental in developing the work described in this book, is a consortium of teachers and post graduate certificate of education (PGCE) tutors in the North East of England dedicated to curriculum development, research and in-service training. It has developed a number of flexible strategies designed to infuse 'teaching thinking' into the geography curriculum (Leat, 1998; Nichols with Kinninment, 2001). One of these strategies, based on an idea developed for co-operative group work (Stanford, 1990) has come to be known as a 'Mystery'. One of these Mysteries that concerns the Kobe earthquake of 1995, is included in the Schools' Curriculum and Assessment Authority's (SCAA, 1996) *Optional Tests and Tasks* publication for key stage 3 teacher assessment. The TTG group has gone on to write many more Mysteries and to research their significance to students' learning.

The use of Mysteries is now widespread in the secondary education sector and to a lesser extent in primary schools. They are being employed as a teaching strategy throughout the curriculum, encouraged by the general recognition of their potential in engaging pupils in collaborative cognitive endeavour and in promoting the full range of thinking skills specified in the National Curriculum (DfEE/QCA, 1999). This has given the development of thinking skills explicit prominence as an educational goal which, along with Assessment For Learning, are central planks of the Key Stage 3 National Strategy for the raising of standards of teaching and learning in the Foundation subjects (DfES, 2002). DfES identifies Mysteries as a versatile and active engagement strategy (DfES, 2003).

This book outlines the use of Mysteries in geography classrooms and reports on research into their use. Our interest in exploring students' thinking and learning was kindled by our own observations and those of the teachers in the TTG group which seemed to suggest that students go through recognisable, observable stages on the way to 'solving' a Mystery. These stages are associated with increasing levels of cognition, and the students' ability to move through these stages is usually reflected in the quality of their explanations. The Structure of Observed Learning Outcomes (SOLO) taxonomy (Biggs and Collis, 1982) provides a framework for analysing the characteristics of students' explanations which can then be related to the stages. Mysteries, then, can provide an insight into how students are thinking. They are valuable diagnostic tools which, once the ways in which students tackle and resolve them are understood, also perform a formative assessment function in that we have some idea of the next steps that students may be able to take, given support. This is meaningful feedback that can help students understand how to advance their thinking.

Mysteries are designed to be group activities and we explore the significance of the social setting to the construction of meaning. We also suggest that through wrestling with Mysteries, students build mental models which they can transfer to other problem solving contexts. Many of those who have used Mysteries in the classroom have been pleasantly surprised by the quality of students' discussions and explanations. Encouraging reflection and evaluation of the ways they tackled a Mystery leads students towards awareness of their own thinking (metacognition) and hence to take greater control of it.

We conclude by acknowledging that we are raising more questions than providing answers. Exploring the factors which contribute to students' abilities to do Mysteries holds the potential for influencing those factors and promoting performance. From the teacher's point of view, observing and interpreting how students tackle Mysteries not only helps open a window to their thinking and learning and provide pointers for scaffolding their progress, it also encourages us to look critically for the intellectual challenge for students in all our teaching.

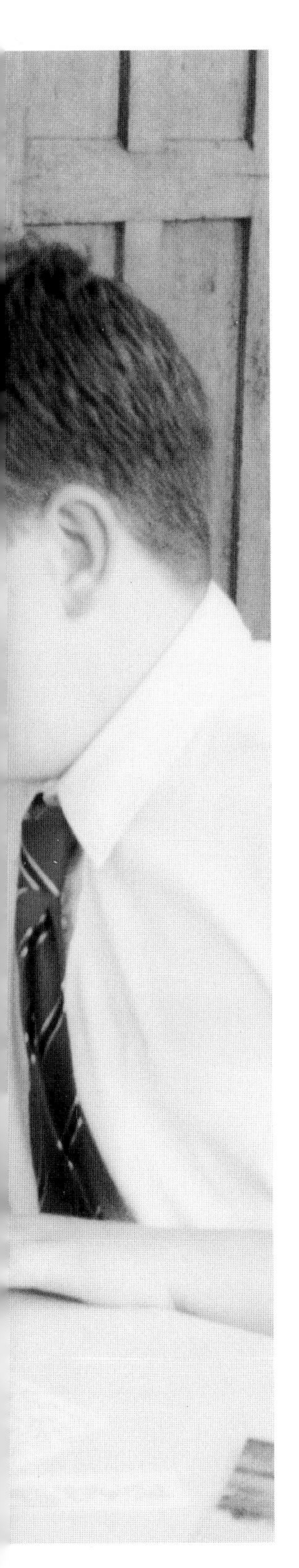

1: Mysteries - what are they?

Mysteries are activities for small groups in which students explore possible explanations for an event. Evidence, in the form of information supplied on 20 to 30 slips of paper, enables a variety of causal relationships to be established which are underpinned by geographical concepts. To solve a 'Mystery' the groups must produce a reasoned argument and support it with evidence contained on the data slips and drawn from their wider understanding of geographical patterns, processes and knowledge.

Mysteries engage students in a wide range of high order thinking skills. These include:

- classification,
- analysis of problems, events and arguments,
- testing of hypotheses,
- speculation,
- inductive and deductive reasoning, and
- the establishment of cause and effect.

In the real world, an event may have a number of contributory causes, some of which trigger it and others (called background factors) which predispose its occurrence. The 'trigger' factors involve concrete, visible phenomena which set events in time and space, while the 'background' factors relate, for the most part, to more abstract geographical generalisations - the relevance of which may not initially be apparent to the students. When constructing a Mystery a strong narrative thread (in which people act and are acted upon) is important for two reasons:

1. it helps engage the interests of students of all abilities, and
2. people's attitudes and behaviours shape events.

Students consider issues from the different perspectives of interested parties and in doing so discover that the significance of some data may be interpreted in more than one way. This element of ambiguity is a conscious ploy to stimulate the critical evaluation of information.

The groups are initially supplied with one central 'open' question to answer, which may be supplemented by 'closed' questions (see, for example, page 19). Students are instructed to sort, arrange and re-arrange the data slips in any manner and as often as they like to help them make sense of the Mystery. The groups are encouraged to use as much of the data as possible in formulating their response to the central question. However, a number of 'red herring' data slips are included, so students must be advised that not all data will be relevant to their answer. (Thus, less able students are not discouraged by the information that they do not at first understand.) Students may not initially consider all the 'red herrings' as irrelevant. Mysteries have more than one 'right' answer so students can use different selections and combinations of data to establish their explanations. If carefully designed, Mysteries are a powerful research tool. They can provide data as valid and reliable as an interview or observation schedule.

Photo: Paula Richardson

2: Writing a Mystery

Writing Mysteries is a creative act and, from our experience, is considerably enhanced by working with a colleague. You should not feel bound by the original source, but should regard it as a starting point. Incorporate as many related geographical concepts and issues as you feel is appropriate for the target key stage with which the Mystery is to be used. You should also keep in mind the expected learning outcomes and the syllabus criteria.

Design principles

Although a number of sources of Mysteries have already been published (Northumberland County Council, 1997; Leat, 1997, 1998) their design is not an exact science. What is important is that you are aware of the design choices that can be made; this will enable you to fully comprehend their learning and research potential. This section outlines the design principles used in the construction of one Mystery and indicates how it could be varied for different contexts and purposes.

The start point for this Mystery was an article 'Can Prescott tame the motor car?' by Patrick Wintour which appeared in *The Observer* (7 June 1998). It was the sort of piece that dedicated geography teachers habitually and dutifully cut from newspapers. You may ask 'But what can be done with it?' - it is rather long, dense and requires a high level of reading ability. Extracts of the article are reproduced in Figure 1 to illustrate three points:

- it contains a lot of valuable information,
- the difficulty of using extracts like this verbatim, and
- to offer an insight into how a Mystery can be generated.

The extract has been used to write the Mystery data slips shown in Figure 2. It has been adjusted as follows:

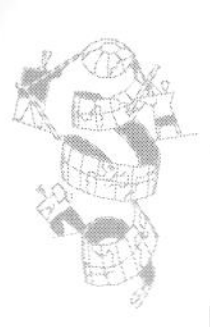

CAN PRESCOTT TAME THE MOTOR CAR?

by *Patrick Wintour*

'This is the crunch moment for John Prescott as Deputy Prime Minister. Unless his Transport White Paper proposes radical action to end the tyranny of the motor car, he will have failed. His reputation, and the whole fate of climate change, is on the line in the next few weeks'. The words were those of the Liberal Democrat leader, Paddy Ashdown, but few at the Department of Environment, Transport and the Regions would disagree.

The Transport White Paper is the first integrated transport strategy for 30 years and will be published in a fortnight.

Armed with polls showing voters will back radical taxes to control the car, but only if money is ploughed back into public transport, Prescott has won his battle with Treasury officials. He insists: *'The British people are in a mood for radical change, and I am in a mood to give it them'.*

As a nation, we now travel 25 miles per person per day, as opposed to 8 miles in the 1950s. On current forecasts, by 2021 urban peak morning traffic will have risen by 36%, traffic on motorways in rural areas will have risen by 88% and on urban motorways by 44%.

By 2016, journey times on urban motorways will have increased by 69% and on rural motorways by a fifth. Gridlock will be the norm, undermining business, the climate and the human spirit. ***Between 1974 and 1996, rail and bus fares have risen by 50 to 75% in real terms, slightly faster than growth in real disposable incomes. The cost of private motoring to the individual, by contrast, has fallen by 3% in real terms.***

On curbing car growth, Prescott will offer sticks and carrots. ***The biggest single growth area is the school run - 20% of peak-hour car journeys are now 'school escort' journeys.*** 'Safe routes for schools' are one idea under consideration.

Local councils seem set to play a major role, preparing traffic reduction plans for central government. Prescott's aides insist they will jump at the opportunity and point to Edinburgh and its transport convenor, David Begg. Begg is planning a £500 million Private Finance Initiative scheme for a rapid transport system. A guaranteed revenue stream to finance investments will come from throwing a ***ring of charges around Edinburgh by 2005 and imposing parking charges on company car spaces.***

Edinburgh says 60% of morning commuter traffic is bound for free parking spaces. The overall aim is to cut city centre traffic by 30% by 2010. *Begg also backs an annual £100 fee for each out-of-town shopping space raising £65 million in Scotland alone. 'The only way to make these charges politically acceptable,' he says 'is to make sure the benefits of better transport come on stream before the charges'.*

1. **A storyline is introduced to act as a hook for students' interest**
   Stories are a cornerstone of our culture (Egan, 1988) and a powerful tool in geography education (McPartland, 1998). Work by Cooper and McIntyre (1995) on students' learning suggests that students attach great importance to personal cognitive engagement with new knowledge.

   Vicki and Raymond are characters around whom an initial explanation can be constructed. The inclusion of 'named individuals' allows the students to draw upon their own knowledge and experience. Although not all households have cars, most students will either have been a passenger in a car or seen such events in the street which will allow them to respond with sympathy or antipathy towards the story. For example:

   - looking for a parking space,
   - preferring the car to the bus for safety or convenience reasons,
   - being taken to school by car,
   - getting clamped or getting a parking ticket, and
   - going to out of town shopping centres.

   Students also gain insights into such issues through watching television programmes (e.g. soap operas or the BBC series *The Wheel Clampers*).

   Many key stage 3 and 4 students may find it difficult to respond to the original newspaper article, both because of its language and abstract nature. Phrases such as 'integrated transport strategy', 'real disposable incomes', 'Private Finance Initiatives' and 'a ring of charges' are linguistically and conceptually challenging. Rooting the learning in a storyline, however, creates the need for the teacher to help students to generalise at some point in order to 'signpost' the geographical concepts involved. Vicki and Raymond are represented in data items 1, 2, 4, 6, 11, 17, 20, 23, 24, 27, 28 and 30.

2. **Abstract information and geographical content**
   Some of the abstract information that provides a context for, and causes of, the issue is taken from the newspaper extract (see emboldened phrases in Figure 1). This represents the geographical content that we would wish the students to understand and can be used to explain why Vicki was clamped (see items 9, 10, 12, 18, 21 and 25). However, items 9 and 12 have been added to widen the spectrum of issues that the students can consider.

3. **Information on possible solutions**
   We have included information about possible solutions to the problem of traffic in towns on the data slips. This is deliberate and allows the Mystery to go beyond the causes and effects of traffic congestion. This design decision also allows greater flexibility in its use (see below). Examples of the solutions are evident in data items 3, 18, 19 and 26.

4. **Peripheral but related concepts**
   We decided to include data items which appear peripheral but are related concepts. These can be used by more able students to construct alternative

Opposite
Figure 1:
A source for a Mystery on traffic management. The emboldened phrases provided some information for the 'Vicki gets clamped' Mystery.

hypotheses or more far-reaching explanations. Thus, we have the suggestions that 'Raymond Storey would not vote Labour if he was not allowed to use his car' in data item 2, while in 16 'the government is worried about inflation', and in 19 that where councils have acted on the issue of transport they risk financial embarrassment (as in Sheffield). You may find that less able students dismiss these peripheral but related data items and some of the genuine ones as 'red herrings'.

5. **Deliberate 'red herrings'**
   The 'red herrings' are included to encourage students to think hard about what information to use. Textbooks tend to present information in a pre-digested form, which requires no mental 'chewing'. In our view this is a crucial cognitive activity, and our experience indicates that students often use this data most imaginatively. In many cases students can justify its inclusion. Here red herring data items include 5, 8, 14, 15, 17 and 27. More complex 'plots' and/or difficult concepts should not include too many red herrings or they will simply confuse rather than challenge the students' thinking. However, what is perceived as irrelevant by students relates to their abilities and levels of pre-existing knowledge. Furthermore, what counts as irrelevant depends heavily on the central question.

The proportion of these design ingredients can be varied depending upon the age group you are teaching. Members of the Thinking Through Geography group have written several Mysteries with no narrative thread for A-level teaching. This is because post-16 students are often able to operate at an abstract conceptual level and do not generally require the same 'hooks' as younger students, though storylines do add to the general enjoyment of the activity.

While you may wish to focus on a particular topic, the potential to inter-relate a variety of concepts from different parts of the syllabus is enormous; for instance, economic geography concepts built into a Mystery on migration or ecosystems as part of a Mystery on agricultural change. Variations in these design principles is one of the research avenues suggested on page 45.

Opposite: **Figure 2:** *The data for the 'Vicki gets clamped' Mystery.*

1 On Saturday 2 July 1998 Vicki Adams returned to her car to find it being clamped.

2 Raymond voted Labour in the last election but won't next time if he is not going to be allowed to drive his Volvo to work.

3 The government is considering charging supermarkets £100 a year for each parking place they provide.

4 Vicki has a Nissan Micra which costs her less in petrol to use than taking the bus.

5 'Buzy Buses' have just had their buses painted yellow and black.

6 Vicki parked in a solicitors firm's parking space.

7 Vicki's brother, Mark, was knocked off his bike on his way to work last year.

8 Dennis Wade, the clamper, replied that he was just doing his job, there was no need to be personal.

9 Climate experts are worried that low-lying countries such as Bangladesh will be affected by the melting of the polar ice caps.

10 Between 1974 and 1996 rail and bus fares have gone up by 50%. The costs of motoring have gone down by 3%.

11 Raymond takes his two daughters to their private school on the way to work.

12 About 10% of school children suffer from asthma.

13 Many people prefer to go to the Metro Centre rather than use their local shops.

14 London requires Heavy Goods Vehicles to have a special licence to use its roads.

15 The value of shares in Stagecoach, the biggest bus company, has gone up a lot in recent years.

16 The government is worried about inflation.

17 Vicki had to pay £100 to have the clamp removed.

18 The Minister of Transport is very keen to reduce car use. He is considering letting Councils charge drivers for bringing cars into town.

19 Sheffield's 'Supertrams' have lost the council a lot of money.

20 Vicki does not feel safe walking home or getting public transport late at night.

21 Many parents are worried about letting their children walk to school.

22 Between a quarter and a third of children are overweight.

23 Vicki had been to pick up her wedding dress with Mark. All the car parks were full in town.

24 Raymond Storey, the solicitor, is fed up with people using his parking space. He employs people to clamp illegal parkers.

25 Some experts say that unless new roads are built, traffic jams will soon be blocking some roads all day long.

26 The government plans to introduce 'super' bus lanes.

27 Vicki called the clamper a 'b*****d' and burst into tears.

28 Raymond always plays golf on Saturday.

29 Since bus services were 'de-regulated' by the Conservatives in the 1980s, city centre roads have become even more congested with almost empty buses.

30 Mark held Vicki up by 10 minutes by going to look for a new CD.

TYNEMOUTH

3: Using Mysteries in the classroom

For teachers and students alike, Mysteries are stimulating and fascinating activities in their own right. However, to use them as a research tool they should be introduced and organised in a manner that allows groups of students to display their own thinking strategies on the desk top.

Preparation

While the data manipulation phase of the Mystery may take between 15 and 25 minutes depending on the number and complexity of conceptual themes and narrative strands, you should allow about 10 minutes for introducing the topic and explaining what to do and upwards of 15 minutes for reporting back and debriefing afterwards. This final phase should not be neglected. It is the point at which the geography embedded in the Mystery should be made explicit. There is a wide range of possible follow-up activities which may be part of the lesson or carried out independently later. Possible activities to consolidate the learning may include group presentations, constructing concept maps, drawing systems diagrams, role plays and extended writing, each requiring different amounts of time. (We consciously did not venture into the variety of possible follow-up activities in the interests of brevity. We wished to focus upon the interpretation of what goes on during the Mystery rather than an evaluation of the successive work, though, admittedly, comparing the quality of the discourse with that of the write-ups is another avenue for further research.)

The data sheet should be photocopied, cut into individual data slips and put into an envelope, one set for each group. Write the central 'open' question on the envelope.

If you want to use a Mystery as a research tool, label each data item with a number or letter so that you can sketch the physical layout of the items at certain points during the lesson.

Some of your students will tackle their first Mystery by trying to put the pieces back into the shape of the original uncut sheet or in a number or letter sequence. Inform them that shapes and markings are of no help in solving the Mystery.

Divide the class into groups of between two and four students and get them to sit in a row. Three abreast is the ideal arrangement - students who are trying to read upside

down are severely disadvantaged. Group composition is at your discretion. Discussion is more readily initiated and less inhibited among friendship groups which, in classes with a broad ability range, tend to be of similar abilities. Many teachers choose this option as it causes minimal fuss. However, many teachers find that allocating students to groups so that the least able are dispersed can have real benefits to their learning (see Chapter 6, page 33-40).

Introducing the task

Give some thought to how you will introduce a class to its first Mystery. If you are using 'Why did Vicki get clamped?' (Figures 1 and 2 - pages 12 and 15) relate an anecdote - perhaps a personal parking or traffic jam nightmare - to get them intrigued. We have found this approach works quite well. Sometimes you can weave stories around an artefact, for example, a fizzy drinks can flattened by vehicles or a photograph of traffic jams, car parks, a clamped car in a city centre or a warden issuing a parking ticket.

While students are free to devise their own strategies for using the data slips to resolve the Mystery, the objectives of the activity must be explicit. The following points will help you to make sure your instructions are as clear as possible.

- The groups should aim to answer the central open question, written on the envelope, and any supplementary closed questions you provide (see below).
- They must also provide a reasoned justification for their answer based upon evidence provided and their own existing knowledge, understanding and experience.
- Encourage the groups to consider all the data in constructing their explanation, to use as many items as they can (but not just for the sake of it) and to lay it out finally in such a way that it helps to shows the structure of their explanation. It is important that the arrangement is not lost as it is a visual prompt for explanation. Blu-Tack can be used to help fix the slips of paper to sugar paper.
- This is a group activity and every member of each group should be able to read the data slips and participate.
- Tell the groups to spread out the slips and scan them for terms that may need clarifying.
- Emphasise that not all the data items are relevant to the answer and that they have to decide what data is unhelpful.
- Reassure the groups that the task is not easy and they will have to work at it. Solving a Mystery takes time and their early conclusions are likely to be challenged as the meaning of other evidence becomes clearer.
- Tell the groups that there are several ways to explain what happened and that you are interested in the quality of their thinking which will be expressed orally to the class at the end of the activity. (It is not necessary to introduce the nature of the follow-up work at this point as it may divert their energies into note-making.)

Student tasks

The first task might be to answer the question 'Why did Vicki get clamped?'. This 'open' question offers much opportunity for differentiation by outcome. And, because of the way this task was constructed, at least three supplementary questions can also be asked:

1. What are the effects of increases in traffic in urban areas?
2. What can be done to reduce traffic in urban areas?
3. Why are some of these solutions difficult to put into operation?

If you are confident that the students will approach the original source with 'advanced organisers' (Ausubel, 1967) (which will allow them to derive more meaning from it than a 'cold' reading), introduce the newspaper extract. The groups should already be familiar with the context and relevant concepts associated with the issues from earlier studies.

One of the advantages of small-group work is that individuals, whatever their ability, are much more likely to air their ideas, think aloud, seek clarification, speculate and contest the meaning of data than they would in a whole-class situation. It is by these means that understanding is constructed and you should not inhibit this free-flowing discourse. Your presence should be as discreet as possible; monitor rather than patrol. Where groups ask you to clarify a technical term (e.g. 'the share price of Stagecoach') or concept, explain it quickly and avoid discussing its wider significance. Very occasionally, because you directed the group formations and some individuals may not be confident or comfortable with each other, a group may be unable to start the task. In such cases kick start the activity by pointing to a key data slip and asking 'Can you find anything that is in some way connected with this?'.

Students will often ask you if the answers they produce are correct. Some individuals will need time to understand that in this case you will accept and even encourage doubt and speculation, and that you will not tell them the 'right' answer. Encourage the group to run through their reasoning so far. If they get stuck, re-launch their thinking (without messing up their arrangements) by simply pointing to a 'redundant' data slip and asking if they think it is connected to any (other) information.

Use your time to listen discreetly and to observe the groups. We would recommend you carry a notebook to record your observations and/or eavesdroppings. This can be of great value in debriefing episodes because it allows you to quote statements or phrases to stimulate reflection, for example, on the steps in thinking that were taken by one group.

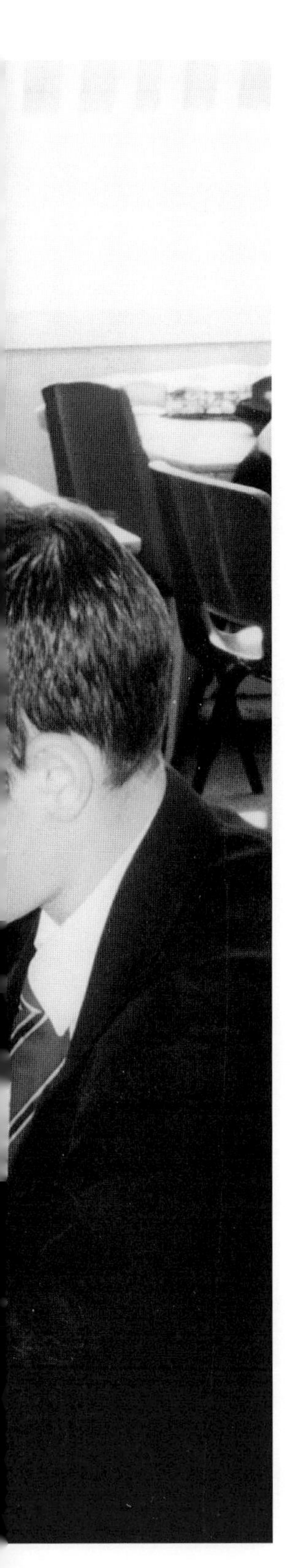

4: Observation and analysis

In the discussions following trials of the 'Kobe Earthquake Mystery', members of the TTG group repeatedly observed a link between the facility with which the students moved the pieces of paper and the quality of the eventual individual written outcome. High ability students/groups were efficient at organising and re-organising the data and their thoughts while lower ability students were often slow and hesitant in finding and imposing any order in the data and would often seek support. (This led some TTG teacher members to provide a set of headings under which the students could organise the data.) This grassroots generalisation allowed us, with the assistance of our classroom colleagues, to speculate about the nature and significance of this relationship. As we watched students physically sorting and organising data on desk tops it began to dawn on us that this manipulation process was a window on cognitive processes and as such a potentially powerful diagnostic tool.

Our aim in the classroom research has been to investigate how students do Mysteries. It is, therefore, naturalistic and has two aspects:

1. What do they physically do with the pieces of paper?
2. What can we infer about the cognitive processes underpinning these physical actions?

In relation to the first aspect we have defined the limits of performance by identifying how Mysteries are tackled by students across the ability range. To explore these questions we have photographed and video-recorded groups doing Mysteries and have made observation notes. Some of the thinking taking place during the Mystery does not, of course, manifest itself physically. In order to try and access this, and to find out what students think they learn from doing Mysteries, we have interviewed the groups and asked how they completed the Mysteries and what they have learned. In some cases we have used stimulated recall by showing the students the video recording of them working.

We have also observed the interactions of teachers with groups. This supplementary concern helps us understand how teachers might most effectively support students within the limitations of the geography classroom. The video recordings have provided valuable evidence in this respect. The use of observation and video in this way is highly innovative; however, student interviews are more firmly established as a research tool and Powney and Watts (1987) offer the best general guidance on their conduct.

Our analysis has taken place in four areas. First, photographs of the students working have been compared with observation notes to delineate phases that students generally go through in physically arranging dataslips. Second, notes and transcripts from student interviews have been compared with phases in data manipulation to calibrate these stages with students' descriptions of their thinking. Third, we have analysed the transcripts of the student interviews for indications that outcomes are being generalised and transferred to other contexts. Fourth, we have watched the videos for evidence of what we (as participant observers) and the teachers did and said when visiting the groups as they worked.

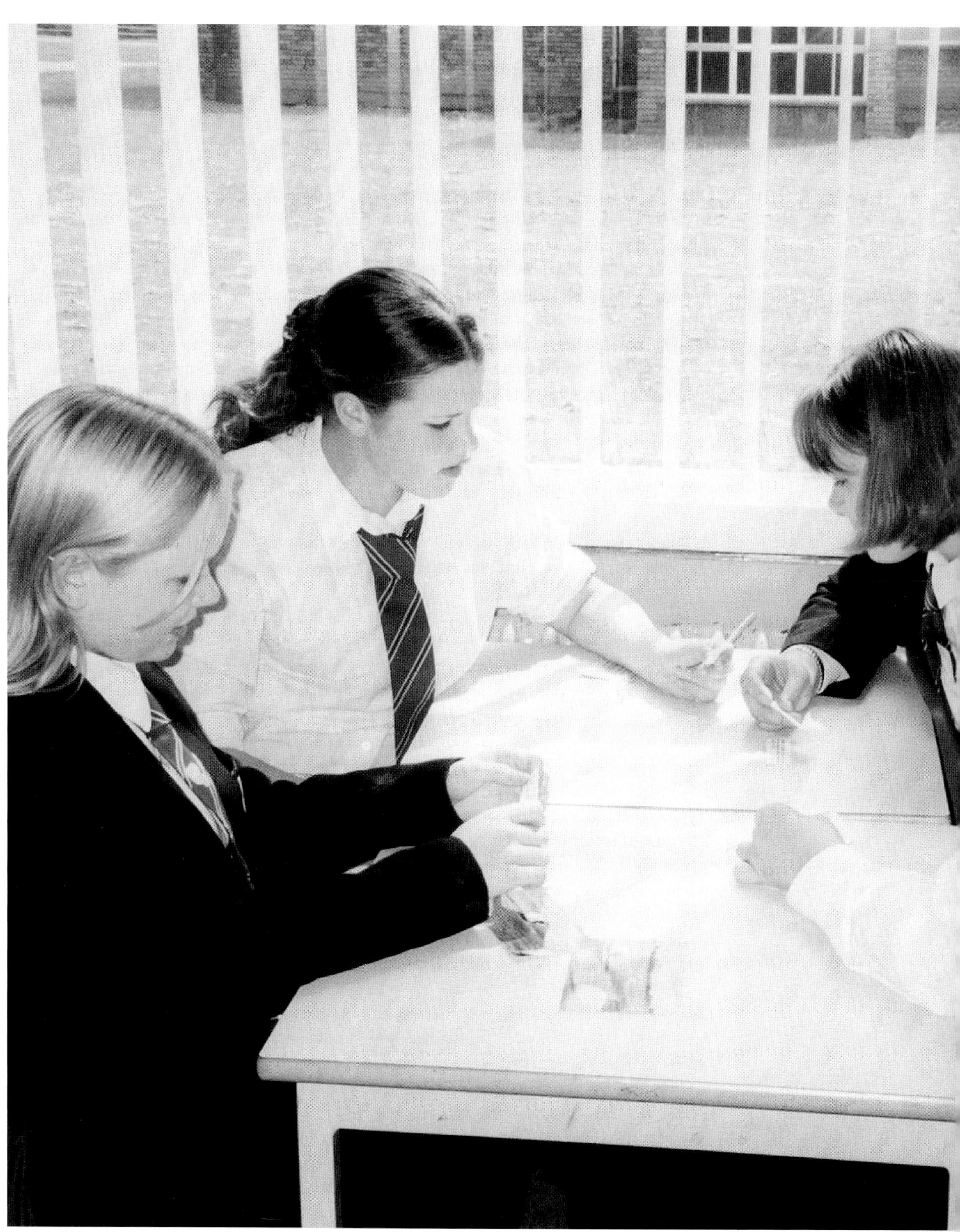

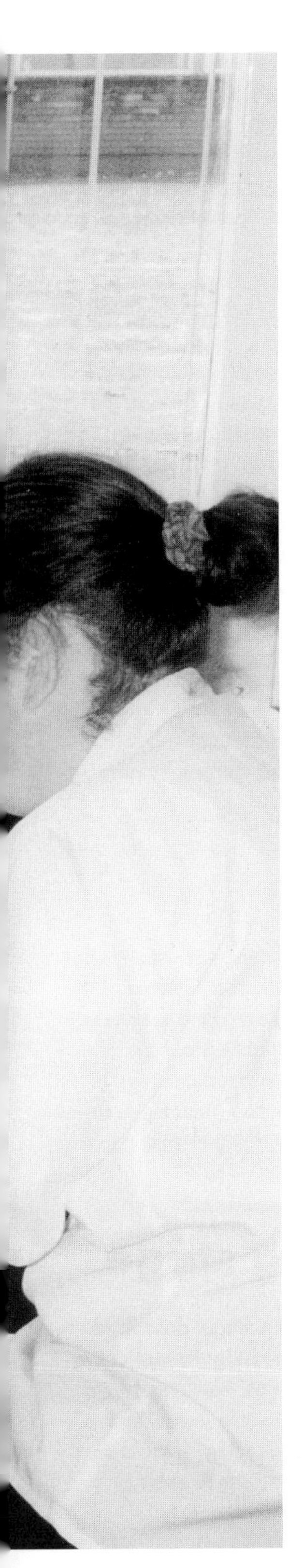

5: Brains on the table?

The analysis revealed a series of physically observable stages that characterise group progression in tackling Mysteries. In many cases (but not all) there were clear breaks between the stages, marked by a very sudden change in the way some of the data was being organised. In some cases group talk indicated a change in thinking before the data slips were moved. We should point out that groups progress through each of the post-display stages in an incremental way. The students tend not to rearrange the data slips wholesale. Some slips from a past arrangement lead the way to the creation of new patterns, reflecting new understanding. Old patterns gradually break up, with residual sets often indicating a concept that the group is unable to integrate into its developing understanding of the big picture.

The display stage

Presented with an unsorted mixture of data slips, not all of which may be useful, the groups familiarise themselves with each item before any further meaningful action can proceed (Figure 3). Some groups elect to distribute the data slips as in a card game to be read aloud before laying them out. Others spread the data slips out either at random or in a neat fashion (Figure 3).

Figure 3:
Display and the emergence of setting.
In the early stages of this mystery about agricultural change, students need to familiarise themselves with the data, usually through displaying it. Two sets are forming here: Large identification letters on each slip help us identify the small group near the student's elbow as a 'common vocabulary' set, each piece containing the name of one of the farming families involved in the plot. The column of five slips is a 'thematic set' which associates EU policy with the character of one of the farms but as yet in no logical order.

The purpose appears to be to allow group members to read the text or at least to register the presence of a data slip that someone else has read aloud (Figure 3). However, some groups do not successfully complete this stage and others accumulate a pile of data slips they have read but have been unable to infer any meaning to (Figure 3). Sometimes individuals hold tightly on to a handful of data slips as if playing a game of cards. Under these circumstances the teacher should kick-start the process as described on page 19.

The setting stage

Inevitably groups are unaware of the relative significance of any particular data slip (remember there is no one definitive 'right' answer). Groups often begin to organise the data into sets on the basis of perceived common characteristics, suggesting a general strategy based on association. Yet even at this early stage groups adopt a variety of strategies which may reflect cognitive ability.

Lower ability groups frequently form sets on the basis of common vocabulary such as the names of characters, animals or places. Many groups assemble broad thematic sets, for example, 'anything to do with earthquakes' or 'data items suggesting a chain of events'. These sets are usually arranged as columns and blocks on the desks. This stage indicates, we believe, a developing familiarity with the events and circumstances. A refinement is the creation of sub-sets, which may be triggered by one thematic set growing so large that the group begins to reclassify them. It is generally the more able groups who form sets based on, or incorporating, the background data, although at this stage they may not appreciate its full significance.

'Reject' set

While sets are being formed, groups encounter some data the significance of which is not yet understood. Consequently, almost all groups initially form a 'reject' pile. Generally, it seems that the number of data slips that each group can attach no meaning to is inversely related to ability. However, a further contrast between less and more able groups is indicated by the fact that the more able groups involve all data bar the 'red herrings' in their final arrangement. This demonstrates that they have returned to their 'reject' pile to reconsider its contents, while some less able groups never look at their 'reject' pile again without prompting by the teacher.

The sequencing and webbing stage

We have observed that some groups do not move beyond the 'setting stage' described above. This is despite the fact that the sets that they have formed may be quite ineffective in terms of producing an explanation or answer. The majority of groups, however, begin to identify relationships between sets or between single data slips. In some instances this is in rows representing the construction of a causal explanation (sequencing) (Figure 4), while in others a non-linear pattern representing multiple inter-relationships (webbing) emerges.

Figure 4: Sequencing.
Slips DD, W and S are a thematic set concerning the CAP while the two central slips are unconnected and represent the remnants of a reject pile. However the three columns represent more than loose associations of ideas. They have been consciously organised into logical sequences which indicate an understanding of causal relationships. Some background data has been incorporated. It is important to note that an understanding of all the concepts embedded in a Mystery is not arrived at simultaneously and that at any one time some data will inevitably be in the previous stage while new arrangements are being formed.

This stage coincides with the first appearance of a coherent hypothesis or an explanation. In connecting concepts the groups are demonstrating an ability to employ reasoning and to reach conclusions about the sub-plots within the narrative. These groups are, in a sense, filling the conceptual spaces or building bridges between the data. Meaning is often inferred in the production of these patterns.

The re-working stage

This stage can be radical or modest and can take many forms. It may start with a group moving one data slip from one set to another, but can go on to add previously rejected slips to a set, or wholesale movement and re-grouping. These re-workings appear to represent the establishment of new sets of relationships, which are increasingly abstract and likely to include some of the background data items that may earlier have been in the 'reject' pile.

Figure 5: Webbing and re-working.
In this unusually imaginative arrangement students have identified three key pieces of information and associated data which represent central concepts of the Mystery between which they have established relationships to make a web of concepts. In this example, students reworked data from sets and sequences to generate the final arrangement.

In the re-working process, data slips which are moved cumulatively take on new meaning. It is our impression that, at this stage, the more the data slips are rearranged, the better the quality of the group's overall understanding of the concepts. We have observed that more able groups show greater willingness to break their original sequences and webs than less able groups which may be very frustrated by having to do so. Reluctance to break patterns may indicate a fear that abstract concepts are understood as long as the visual prompts exist; however the group may not have assimilated the concept adequately to retain it after the slips have been re-worked.

The abstract stage

A few groups cease the physical manipulation of slips, but continue their discussion. In such cases it is possible that the group has internalised the concept to a point where they can explore new relationships and hypotheses without recourse to the concrete format of the data slips.

An example

Below are extracts from an interview with a group of fairly able girls to illustrate the stages outlined above. The girls have done a Mystery focused on stock losses from an organic farm. The extracts are interspersed by our comments on what stages and skills are being evidenced. As we should be cautious in inferring cognitive processes from stimulated recall interviews, you would be well advised to treat our commentary as hypothesis. (Names have been changed.)

Interviewer: So what are you doing here?
Kate: We're just sort of reading them - seeing what they were.
Commentary: This is the display stage. The dominant process is comprehension of the data items.

Interviewer: What's that little grouping there?
Sara: It was the Leythorpe hunting things - linking those together ... but we read most of them first .... We tried to put them into little groups that linked together.
Jodie: And the hedgerows and stuff.
Kate: And we thought that the golfers on Massey's Farm would be complaining [about the smell from the organic farm].
Commentary: The group is in the setting stage. However, before they finish this stage they start to make links that are characteristic of webbing. They are using classification skills, deciding on what is relevant and already looking for relationships between the data.

Interviewer: There's a new [set] beginning there ... What's happening there?
Kate: That's the one where we didn't know which one ... but I think it was the herbicides and pesticides and that.
Interviewer: Was that because you didn't know what they did?
Kate: Yeah and we were a bit lost.
Commentary: A new thematic set is formed, the significance of which is not initially apparent. However, they now begin to make substantial progress as they make connections characteristic of the sequencing and webbing stage.

Kate: But then we found the fact about the steep decline in birds and then we linked that together with the pesticides and herbicides and the fact that they ate little bugs ... that used to destroy the crops, then when the bugs were killed then the birds wouldn't have much to eat.
Jodie: Plus the hedgerows were getting destroyed and their nests getting destroyed as well.
Commentary: By establishing these relationships, they were linking sets in a logical

causal sequence and at the same time weaving in some of the background data. They are generating hypotheses in the process. This group was able to use a wider range of data than some other groups in the class.

Interviewer: This is clearly becoming a very important category. You are doing all the talking here.

Kate: I'm just saying that if the birds are being poisoned .... the chickens ... they would have found the bodies unless the fox had eaten them but then you'd have found feathers.

Commentary: However, at this point the majority of slips were still in three sets, which did not particularly help in the construction of an explanation, and frustration had set in. The abandonment of the original sets is a turning point as they then re-work the data items and adopt a new strategy leading to a very different understanding.

Jodie: We started to get stuck. We just like completely gave up for two minutes because it wasn't working, got bored, then got back into it when we decided to split the groups up.

Sara: We split them all up. We took one then looked to see which ones linked to that.

Jodie: One of them was about the EMU, quotas and everything, we put them in a group, ... encouraging people to get rid of hedgerows and stop them growing so much.

Commentary: This group shows great flexibility in being prepared and able to destroy their original explanatory structure and start again. This is greatly assisted by the very fact that they can move the pieces of paper around. It is worth recognising the part that emotions played here - they got stuck and bored and gave up temporarily. In their explanation of looking for new links they are demonstrating an ability to evaluate possibilities. In addition, the students show that they are able to assimilate abstract concepts (embodied in the background data) about the Common Agricultural Policy into their explanation, in a way that other groups in the same class were not.

Diagnostic and formative assessment

The pattern emerging above bears close resemblance to the SOLO taxonomy proposed by Biggs and Collis (1982). Their work was empirically derived from analysing the work of hundreds of students of different ages and across a range of subjects. Biggs and Collis (1982) detected a recurring pattern which they described in five levels - Prestructural, Unistructural, Multistructural, Relational and Extended abstract. The SOLO taxonomy resonates with the Piagetian stages of cognitive development. While the SOLO taxonomy classifies the range of students' responses to a particular task at a particular time, Piaget also considered the sequential development of cognition in individuals over time. The coincidence of the observed stages and the SOLO taxonomy gives greater credence to the proposal that research using Mysteries reveals important cognitive processes. The relationship of SOLO stages to those of the Mystery stages we have observed are described overleaf.

Prestructural responses do not address the question or task set. Answers at best may simply re-state the question. Those groups who, if left unaided can make no sense of the data in relation to the question, could be considered to be showing a prestructural response.

Unistructural responses use one piece of relevant data in a descriptive mode without a conclusion related to the data. The unistructural responses can be matched to the 'Display stage', where data items, individually, are being tested for relevance.

Multistructural responses use two or more pieces of data, but without linking them strongly. The closest correspondence is to the 'Setting stage', where the linkage between data items can be very tentative.

Relational responses are qualitatively different from those described above. Here the student links the data together in a coherent manner and reaches a conclusion consistent with the data. There is a correspondence with the 'Sequencing and webbing stage', where students are moving towards theories and explanations, in which data items are tentatively threaded into an explanation.

Extended abstract responses are characterised by the inclusion of data not given in the task, by the creation of abstract concepts and the consideration of a number of competing hypotheses. This bears a resemblance to the 'Re-working' and 'Abstract' stages.

Do Mysteries have a task structure and student response that will allow teachers to employ diagnostic and formative assessment processes which substantially aid learning? Figure 6 outlines some of our observations during the use of Mysteries in relation to this question. These may indicate that students have reached stumbling blocks which impede their progress towards understanding and explaining the Mystery. A diagnostic interpretation of this observation and what the teacher might do in a formative mode as a consequence is shown below.

Wood and Wood (1996) are among a number of authors who have attempted to operationalise Vygotsky's (1978) theoretical concept of the Zone of Proximal Development (ZPD). The ZPD refers to the gap between what a child can achieve alone and what he or she can achieve through problem solving under adult guidance, or in collaboration with more able peers. The term 'scaffolding' was coined by Wood, Bruner and Ross in 1976. They explored the guidance role that adults (not necessarily teachers) might play and identified several potential tutoring functions. These include the following five points.

1. Recruiting the child's interest.
2. Establishing and maintaining an orientation to task-related goals.
3. Highlighting critical features that a child might overlook.
4. Demonstrating how to achieve goals.
5. Helping to control frustration - to avoid at one extreme a child being left to struggle with too much complexity and at the other having too little scope for involvement.

In terms of classroom teaching using Mysteries, a successful introduction using a story is coterminous with recruitment of the child's interest (point 1). In addition, giving clear instructions can establish and maintain orientation to task-related goals (point 2). (For example, one of the instructions for the students is that not all of the information is pertinent and they have to decide on its relevance to the Mystery.) Highlighting critical features that a child might overlook (point 3) premises the same knowledge base as diagnostic assessment, namely an analysis of the cognitive or physical demands of a task. In terms of supporting students' progress, the kick starts and re-starts described on page 19 fulfil this tutoring role. Point 4 mirrors formative assessment in providing feedback that will inform future action; and point 5 combines points 3 and 4.

The term 'scaffolding', as used by Wood *et al.* (1976), involves both diagnostic and formative assessment. Appropriate teacher intervention (scaffolding) is dependent upon an analysis of student progress (diagnostic assessment) and an appreciation of productive next steps in order to achieve task goals (formative assessment). In their discussion on dynamic assessment, Brown and colleagues assert that:

> 'Tests that provide information about what a child does not know now but is just about ready to learn would be invaluable to a classroom teacher' (Brown *et al.*, 1992, p. 123).

Mysteries have the potential to be invaluable in indicating some aspects of what students cannot do at the moment and how they might be helped to take their next educational steps.

If teacher assessment is to demonstrate its importance it must develop a distinctive function beyond simple measures of accountability and it must also be accepted as valid. We note that validity is a contested concept, but find much encouragement in Wiliam's proposal that 'a test is valid to the extent that one would be happy for teachers to teach towards the test' (Wiliam, 1992, p. 17). Using this as a yardstick, we would argue that Mysteries represent a profile of validity that more traditional tests lack.

Figure 6:
Observation of student difficulties at each stage, diagnostic interpretation and possible action.

Stage	Observation	Possible meaning Diagnostic assessment
Display	Students cannot start	Inability to read data items
		Inability to comprehend
Setting	Inability to group data items	Inability to identify more important characteristics that would inform classification
Sequencing and webbing	Setted data unsorted	Inability to draw upon prior knowledge
	Line of data items	Inability to identify sequence events or causal relationship
	Isolated groups	Causation seen as a simple linear sequence or causal chain
		Unable to make links betwe factors/sets
Reworking	No reworking	Reluctance to reconsider alternatives
	Reject pile ignored	Reluctance to reconsider alternatives
	Bizarre theories	Lack of critical evaluation
Abstract	No reference back to data	Over-generalisation or lack critical evaluation

ssible action rmative assessment
erence to Special Needs ordinator
plify text
students: 'What do you k this means?'
ntify a characteristic of a a item and ask 'Can you me another that is to do n X?'
resh memory of past eriences or learning
'Do you think this ppened before or after that?' ny?'
nsult reject pile for key data ask 'Do you think this ce might help?' te students to connect a a item to a point along the ar sequence
'Is there any link between group and that one?'
estion logic or invite one up to compare with another
g selected items from reject to their attention
questions such as: 'So you arguing ...?' 'How likely is it ...?' allenge them to justify bring specific data slips
for explanations of cepts that have been ored or avoided er students back to data to ck theory

Figure 6 outlines the way in which a teacher can 'teach towards the test', in a contingent manner (Wood and Wood, 1996), i.e. not seeking to generate a right answer, but supporting the development of certain cognitive skills that most teachers would agree are important in becoming an effective learner.

Brown and colleagues sum up the position rather neatly in saying 'Ideally, children are not labelled and categorised by assessment, they are diagnosed and helped' (Brown *et al.*, 1992, p. 190). Following Black and Wiliams' (1998) major review of the role of assessment in supporting learning, as opposed to labelling, teachers of all subjects need urgently to develop and refine new tools for the diagnostic and formative modes of assessment. Mysteries, we suggest, can be such a tool.

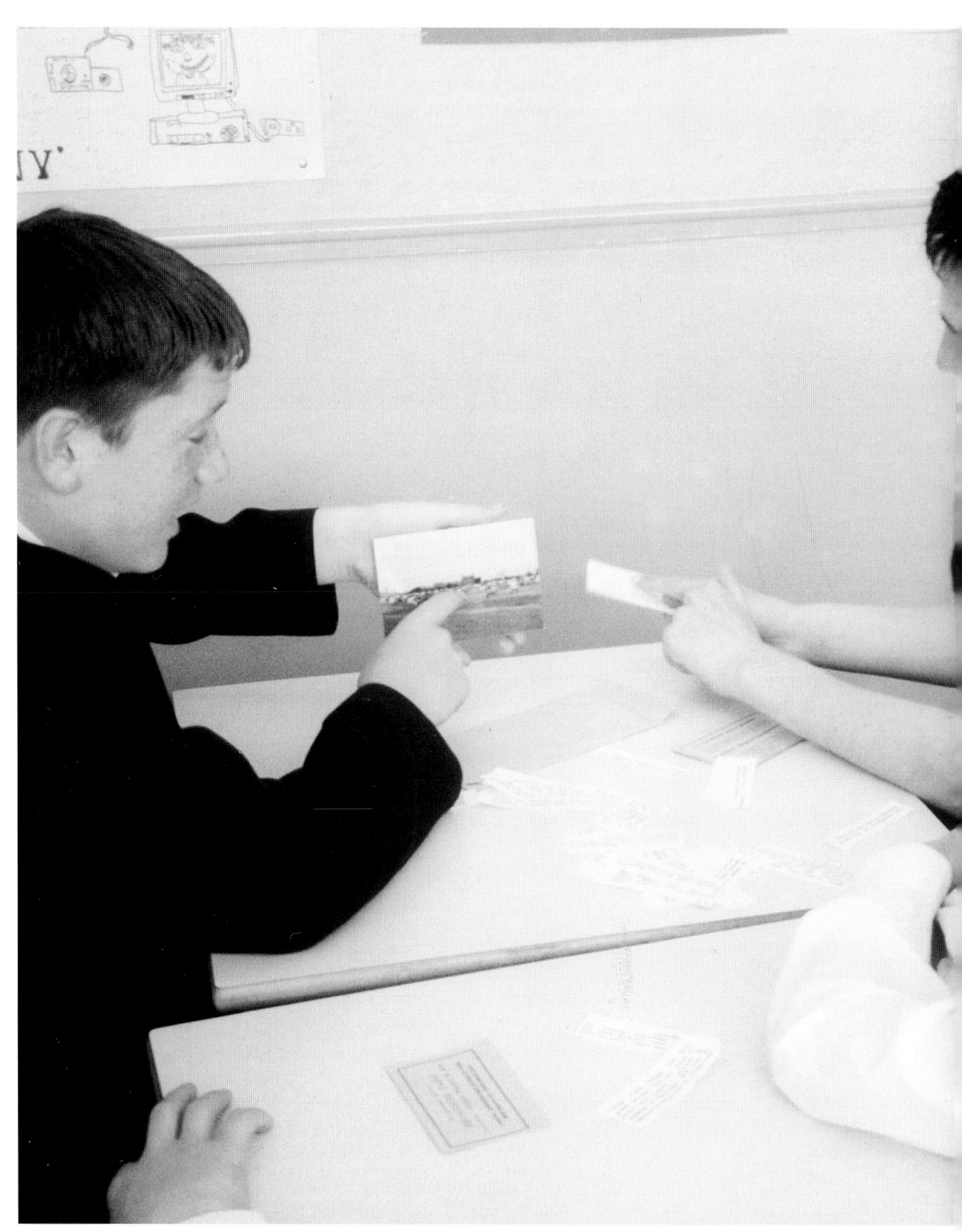

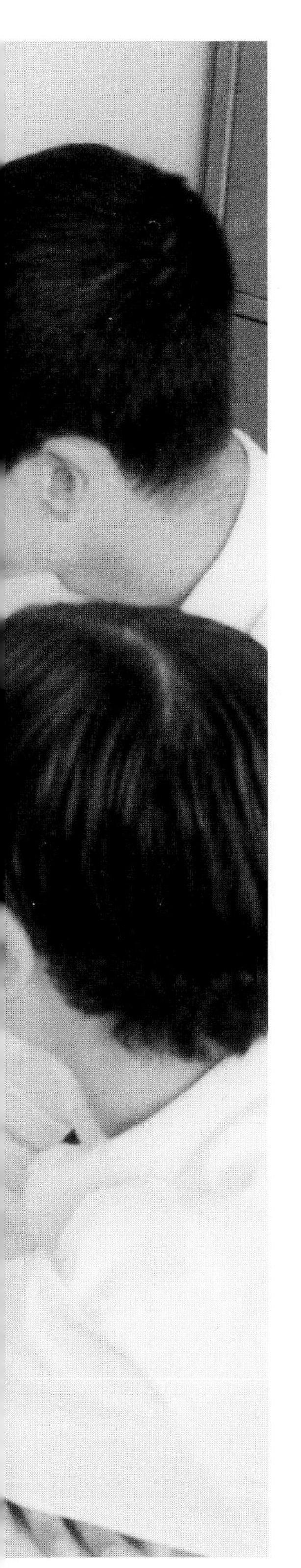

6: What and how do students learn from Mysteries?

We feel it is important to provide some analysis of what students might learn through doing Mysteries and highlight some of the conditions that underpin the learning outcomes. Colleagues have pointed out that the immediate outcomes do not always appear to be strongly related to geography, and imply that this casts a shadow over the place of Mysteries in a subject-based curriculum. We would like to respond to this criticism in three ways. First, as with any well-structured geography lesson, the activity should always be followed by a debriefing/recapping phase in which the geography involved in the Mystery can be made explicit. Second, the follow-up tasks can focus on the key geographical concepts that were embedded in the Mystery at the design stage. Third, Mysteries that are not based directly upon factual events are nonetheless analogous to them. The Mystery can be said to mediate geographical understanding and serve an illustrative and explanatory function in the same way as a story, an anecdote or a case study.

Construction and social construction

The current dominant learning paradigm is constructivism. In simple terms we learn largely, though not exclusively, through what we already know. Our existing knowledge structures are described as schemata. If incoming information makes no sense in terms of what we already know, it will be lost. An effective way of appreciating this is to consider a radio broadcast on a football match, which might go as follows:

> 'Watson threads a neat ball inside the full back, Lee is on to it, he hits it across first time and there is Shearer getting in front of his marker at the near post with a great flick, but Seaman stands up really well and keeps it out at the expense of a corner.'

If you have played and watched football and listened to commentaries before, this passage makes some sense. However, those of you who have managed to avoid football all your life will not have schemata which will assist with the decoding of the description 'Watson threads a neat ball inside the full back' or 'Seaman stands up really well'! Schemata come from experience.

A renewed interest in the work of Vygotsky (1978) has led educators to recognise that construction of meaning is not just a solo activity, it is usually undertaken with others through talk in social settings. Wertsch (1985), Moll (1990) and Mercer (1992) are among the many researchers who have emphasised the collaborative nature of learning, where meaning is jointly constructed and is heavily influenced by context. If we accept that one of the common weaknesses of classroom teaching and learning is that students are not encouraged to use their existing knowledge in understanding new material, then Mysteries offer some salvation. In order to make use of a data item students must understand it. At the 'Setting stage' (page 24), in particular, students may place a considerable amount of data which they do not understand on their 'reject' pile. Watch and listen to them in the early stages of a Mystery and you will almost certainly witness the joint construction of meaning based on existing knowledge of the different members of a group. It is fascinating to gain an insight into the knowledge that students bring to these tasks. Mercer (1992) argues that what counts as context for students is whatever they consider relevant, and the context they create consists of the knowledge they invoke to make sense of the task. We would emphasise that it is the absence of a self-evident solution in Mysteries combined with the ambiguity of some of the data that leads students into constructive talk. Or, as White puts it, the 'slight aura of fuzziness and confusion that is always the backdrop to real communication' (White, 1989).

The 'Setting stage' in Mysteries encourages students to go beyond the literal meaning of the data. Their physical movement of the data slips correlates with the students attaching cumulatively increasing meaning to each item. In the latter stages of 'solving' a Mystery, students use inference - both interpolating and extrapolating beyond the data, which may be based upon existing knowledge and experience. However, to do so students must accept the task as genuinely open and not an elaborate trap. Mason (1996) draws on the work of, for example, Brown and Campione (1990) and Pontecorvo (1990) to focus on the importance of using argument in class. During this 'argument', students are called upon to give explicit reasons, explanations and justifications. In the process of such collaborative endeavour conceptual change is likely to occur as students distance themselves from their own beliefs and entertain others' perspectives. Evidence from video recordings of group discussions in mixed ability groups indicates that Mysteries provide a context within which the more able are supporting the construction of meaning by the less able. It is possible to over-simplify this relationship because Mysteries encourage active participation by students who are poor at writing but who have good verbal reasoning skills, so it is not always clear who is more and who is less able. By moving a data slip to form part of another set, the student must explain and justify a causal chain or a link between factors to their group. Their reasoning has to be externalised thus creating the conditions for shared reasoning. The following extract, taken from a group of able year 9 students who have done a Mystery concerning pressures on Lake District farmers, highlights this process. (The students are aware that the pressures on farmers have led one to commit suicide.)

Emma: We had the cards that we were using and we set them out into groups and once we heard different peoples' cards we found out that they had some cards that we didn't have in our group.
Interviewer: You actually changed your mind?
All students: Yeah.

Interviewer: So can you remember any examples of things you changed your minds on?
Supriya: The four generations part [the fact that one family had farmed the particular farm for four generations].

[later in the interview]

Nathan: Sometimes you only think of one thing and you don't think anybody else is right, then when somebody explains, they explain their view, it makes you think about it.

This snippet illustrates a feature of much of our research into Mysteries. Small-group and whole-class discussions help students exchange ideas. Within this process, they change their minds, but more importantly they build on each other's ideas, fusing their thoughts with those of others to create new meaning. This is further illustrated in the following extract.

Fay: It's better to have someone else's opinion.
Interviewer: Why? I don't think that you are wrong; I want to know why?
Fay: Because you can put your ideas and their ideas together and make it, like, better.
Interviewer: Why is it important to talk about your ideas? If you and I sat down now and talked about our opinions or some of our ideas, why is that better than you deciding on your own?
Fay: You can find out better ideas than you had and make them better ... and make them more exciting and more serious.

The social context is, therefore, crucial to what is learned. The learning is embedded in the activity and it is from the activity that rich understanding of concepts emerge. Brown *et al.* (1989) emphasise that the meaning of a concept continuously evolves with each new occasion of use. They stress that, because application recasts meaning, 'a concept, like the meaning of a word, is always under construction' (Brown *et al.*, 1989, p. 34). Concepts which arise inductively from the students' work as they group the data items are likely to be more powerful than those which are encountered through a decontextualised transmission process. The extract on pages 26-27 provides evidence of a group of girls constructing extended understanding of the concept of ecosystems.

Mental models

Mental models nest within constructivist theory. Hatano and Inagaki (1992) use learning to cook to illustrate the importance of mental models. They assert that as novice cooks we are highly dependent on external support (such as a recipe in a book) and on having all the right ingredients and utensils. If something is missing or a few lines of the recipe are obliterated, we are stumped. We progress through a stage of remembering recipes, thus using acquired knowledge, but this knowledge does not transfer in that we cannot interchange some parts of recipes. However, Hatano and Inagaki describe a further

stage that is qualitatively different when we acquire conceptual knowledge 'which means more or less comprehensive knowledge about the nature of the objects and of the procedures (i.e. what they are like)' (Hatano and Inagaki, 1992, p. 116). If conceptual knowledge is flexible in the sense that it changes in response to thinking it is referred to as a mental model:

> 'When we possess a mental model of the target object we can understand the meaning of each step of a given procedure in terms of the change it produces in the object. By running the mental model we can also predict what will occur in situations that have not been experienced' (Hatano and Inagaki, 1992, p. 116).

Mental models, therefore, suggest a way in which knowledge learned in one context can be de-situated and applied to another. Gentner and Stevens (1986) and Halford (1993) also emphasise that mental models are generative, i.e. they allow predictions to be made. Mental models can assist recall because they act as a prompt and thus reduce the amount of information that needs to be rote learned (e.g. 'What was the trigger in this situation?' is a prompt that can help recall).

Do Mysteries supply a context in which students can develop mental models? And, if they do, what supports this development?, and what is the form of the mental model?. The following extract, while not providing conclusive evidence, offers a tentative response to these questions. This is a group of more able year 9 students who have just done a Mystery on farming in the Lake District.

Interviewer: OK, if we go back to thinking about what you've learned, can we pin that down. Is there anything about geography?

Ellen: I wouldn't say that we've learned anything specific today, it's like we're relearning things that we've done in the past, that we've been learning over the two years.

Interviewer: Such as?

Ellen: Background and trigger.

Interviewer: Background and trigger. Right. Is that useful? You're not going to get a question in a geography examination that says ...

Joanna: In projects and stuff. It can help you.

Ellen: For writing essays and stuff, you have all the reasons, background and trigger reasons, it can help you sort of arrange an essay and write it.

Joanna: And if you are going to college you can use it. I think this happened because of background.

[later in the interview]

Interviewer: Do you think your other work, in any other subjects has improved because of that.

Ellen: Geography and history, you use the same skills that you learn.

Carmel: And like in English, we're doing like an AT on listening. We've got to do like a debate, and doing background and trigger that will help for that as well.

This extract indicates that some of these students are de-situating their learning. What they have learned about farming in the Lake District is overshadowed by what they have learned about causation (and handling data, decision making, discussion, etc.). The students know, for example, that in many situations, including analysing the play *Macbeth* in English, they can look for trigger and background factors and use this framework to structure their writing. They also know that in certain types of episodes there will be a chain of events which include a trigger (or triggers) and that these triggers are different in different episodes. The students can use this model to make predictions, for example, if certain background conditions are changed some episodes are much less likely to occur and others become more so. There is much more to learn about causation, relating to probability, trends, strength and classification of factors. The danger here is that this becomes distilled into a rigid set of algorithms about causation that students have to learn in geography.

Work in the USA has shown that more able students require less help to transfer rules and principles to novel problems. This relative advantage grew as the transfer distance (the degree of un-relatedness of the novel context) increased (Brown *et al.*, 1992). Mental models are implicated in students' ability to transfer rules and principles, especially in what Perkins and Salomon (1988) term 'high road routes' where the task goes beyond applying a procedure or algorithm to a similar problem. As students become more proficient at organising and classifying data in Mysteries, their confidence in hypothesising and speculating increases. They construct models of the Mystery process itself and then transfer this knowledge to new contexts in geography and other subjects.

Literacy

Mysteries involve speaking, especially exploratory talk, and listening, interacting with text and usually writing in follow-up activities. As such they can make a significant contribution to developing literacy. Wray and Lewis (1997) describe the Extending Interactions with Text (EXIT) model which has been developed to represent the processes underlying student learning from non-fiction text. The EXIT model has ten stages (see Figure 7).

Figure 7: *The ten stages of the EXIT model.*

1 Activating previous knowledge.
2 Establishing purposes.
3 Locating information.
4 Adopting an appropriate strategy.
5 Interacting with text.
6 Monitoring understanding.
7 Making a record.
8 Evaluating information.
9 Assisting memory.
10 Communicating information.

The extract shown on page 38 is taken from an interview with a group of mixed ability year 10 students after they had completed a Mystery. The Mystery allowed them to compare the effects of one hurricane on three areas in the Caribbean and eastern United States. The extract provides evidence that Mysteries can have a profound catalytic effect in promoting interaction with text, which is epitomised in the student's phrase, 'If you are just reading it you hardly take much in'.

At least half of the EXIT stages (1, 4, 5, 6 and 8) are strongly represented in the Mysteries stages we have described (see pages 23-26). Chall *et al.* (1990) provide intriguing evidence on how some American children (mainly from low income families) fall behind in reading scores. The children show slippage on tests of word meaning – especially abstract

Interviewer: Right ... so if Mr K had given you the information in a big paragraph, like a page in a textbook and told you to compare ...
Alistair: It would have been boring.

[later in the interview]

Rachel: If you are just reading it you hardly take much in, but it's like a practical, you get more ...
Interviewer: So you actually need holding and moving things?
Rachel: Yeah. Because if it's in the book you can't rip the book apart and put them in order.
Interviewer: So that helped? Even though you had to have bits of card .. and bits of paper, that would have been quicker than giving you the set exercise?
Rachel: [Emphatically] Yes.

literary and less common words. Greenhough and Hughes (1998) have speculated that this 'slippage' may be attributed to a lack of opportunity to converse about texts. Language and cognition, which are rooted in talking about text to make meaning, become stronger predictors of reading scores than word recognition and phonics. We would argue that Mysteries have a role to play in encouraging comprehension of important geographical vocabulary. Moreover, students tend to use this vocabulary more readily and confidently on subsequent occasions.

Mysteries may also be used to encourage writing. Through the physical manipulation and positioning of data slips meaningful associations are established by the students and these can provide frameworks for written explanations. The SCAA (1997) discussion paper *Extended Writing in Key Stage 3 History* provides examples (albeit using tasks that are not strictly Mysteries) of how this might be approached. Forms of Mystery can also be found in use in the key stage 3 National Strategy training materials for Literacy across the curriculum (DfEE, 2001).

Cognitive skills

Feuerstein (1980) has developed a programme called Instrumental Enrichment (IE) which seeks to improve cognitive skills or functions through modules or instruments. Feuerstein's work draws on Vygotsky's view that thinking is a cultural artefact transmitted through social processes from adults to children. IE is founded on the principle of mediated learning in which the adult assists the child learner in interpreting the task and making sense of the thought processes employed in tackling it. Feuerstein argues that for most lower ability students the problem is not a lack of intelligence but a lack of cognitive functions. An absence of mediation has resulted in these students failing to develop cognitive functions and thus they are culturally deprived. IE distinguishes between three groups of functions – input of information, using the information (elaboration) and output (expressing solutions) (Feuerstein, 1980). Examples of these functions are shown opposite.

Elaboration functions

- Using only the part of the information we have gathered that is relevant, i.e. that which applies to the problem, and ignoring the rest (relevance).
- Having a good picture in our mind of what we are looking for or what we must do (interiorisation).
- Looking for the relationship by which we can tie together separate objects, events, and experiences (projecting relationships).
- Finding the class or set to which the new object or experience belongs (categorisation).
- Thinking about different possibilities and figuring out what would happen if we were to choose one or another (hypothetical thinking).
- Using logic to prove things and to defend our opinion (logical evidence).

Output functions

- Carrying an exact picture of an object in our minds to another place for comparison without losing or changing some details (visual transport).

Instrumental Enrichment represents a pole in teaching thinking programmes, in that it emphasises procedural skills in thinking, with little attention to conceptual knowledge. This is deliberate because the natural client group has repeatedly been unsuccessful within the disciplines of the school curriculum. The 'content' of IE bears no relation to any school subject and the subject matter has been described as abstract and decontextualised in order to provide a fresh start for those students who associate certain school subjects with failure. Clearly IE has 'content', because it is not possible to think about nothing; rather the emphasis is on cognitive functions. Our interview extracts provide evidence that Mysteries offer students substantial opportunities to develop and refine many of the cognitive functions listed above. Further evidence is provided by the following extract.

Interviewer: What do you think you learnt during that lesson?
Sam: We learnt ... like looking at these different cards, we learnt how to read them all and put them into groups ...
Debbie: We learnt how to look into information, like you get one piece of information ...
Rebecca: And put it into lines and stuff.
Alex: We learnt how to group things together and see what might affect other things and then clues ...
Debbie: Like one thing starts another.

Metacognition

Metacognition is an elusive concept which has undergone what has been termed 'construct creep' since Flavell coined the term in 1977. Flavell describes metacognition as representing knowledge of one's own cognitive processes and products including active monitoring and consequent regulation and orchestration of these processes. Its essence concerns the conscious management of thinking.

The following interview involves two very able year 9 girls from another school doing the Kobe Earthquake Mystery. There are strong similarities in the pattern of the stages, however, a number of points of difference are worth noting. First, although they were aided by the manipulation of data slips, these girls never appeared to be as dependent on it for the development of their thinking. Second, they were quicker to form thematic groups in the 'Setting stage' (page 24). Third, the girls were able to be much more explicit about the strategies that they employed in trying to impose order on the data slips (though readers should bear in mind that this may be *post hoc* rationalisation). And fourth, they demonstrated impressive evidence of transfer of learning from other contexts in this process. Our hypothesis is that these students are managing their thinking as they try to use 'storyboarding' as an organising framework: however, they abandon it because they cannot accommodate background (abstract) factors. The girls switch to sorting data into groups, using reliability of evidence as a filter.

Interviewer: You have one at the top there about Japan being a rich country?
Beth: It was like a background [the interviewer and the teacher had not used this word]. It was not in order, it was background, Japan is a rich country and the plates stuff, it's not in any order.
Interviewer: You are forming groups?
Both girls: Yes.
Beth: I thought that they should end up in a line like a storyboard, but they didn't all go [storyboards had not been mentioned].
Interviewer: Where have you used storyboards?
Both girls: In English.
Interviewer: What didn't fit?
Beth: The backgrounds.
Amrita: There were the buildings and things that contributed to her death, but not directly.
Interviewer: Have you done background before?
Amrita: [looking at Beth] Once or twice in year 8. We did not realise that we were doing it. New things kept cropping up and things changed ... so it changed. We were looking at evidence and sorting and re-sorting.
Interviewer: Have you looked at evidence before?
Both girls: In history.
Amrita: In history we do sources, which sources are reliable and which are unreliable.

Mysteries provide an inviting practice ground for the development of metacognitive awareness, control and self-regulation for three reasons:

1. They are open tasks which allow a broad range of strategies to be employed in sorting the data and building explanations. Students have a real choice about the route they take, so they have something which can be reflected upon.
2. The physicality of the data manipulation allows their strategies to be observed.
3. The physical manipulation invites students to alter explanations and reasoning - by moving a data slip the student has some automatic control over strategy. Students are encouraged to think again.

The option to 'think again' may be one of the most important ground conditions for metacognition because it allows for what is termed 'executive control', which Brown (1978) proposes as the essence of intelligent activity. Nisbet and Shucksmith (1986) analogise learning in terms of information technology, with hardware representing ability, software as the procedural skills we have learned and the operator of the system as metacognitive executive control.

Opening
your eyes
to Europe

7: Conclusion and ways forward

Mysteries can provide opportunities for geography teachers to teach and for students to learn in ways which make the subject come alive. In essence their importance is as much to do with understanding and advancing the students' processes of thinking as with the content of geography. The importance of 'thinking through geography' is, therefore, highlighted within the Mysteries that have been designed so far. As one of the aims of Mysteries is for students to become more independent in their learning and more questioning of the content that is placed before them, this aspect has particular importance. We realise that using Mysteries within your teaching implies a process of professional development and change, but it is only through you taking risks, understanding more about the ways in which your students learn and altering your current classroom practices that the techniques described here will be successful.

Although there is no definitive structure to each Mystery those described in this book tend to conform to certain principles of design. They involve students working in small groups seeking to explain the reasons for a particular event; this event has some form of geographical expression. Students are provided with a variety of pieces of information about the event on separate data slips - these may contain overtly geographical material, background data or contextual information, or may even include content which is peripheral but related to the event itself. In many Mysteries a strong narrative thread often helps students maintain a stronger attachment and engagement with the new material. Each Mystery has a central 'open' question (and supplementary 'closed' questions) for the group to pursue. In seeking an explanation the group will have to produce a reasoned argument to support their views, using both the information provided by the data slips and their own background knowledge and understanding of geographical patterns and processes. Through their arrangement and re-arrangement of the data slips each group will attempt to solve the Mystery. It is this very process which provides the teacher, and the students themselves, with important indicators of the ways in which thinking is being advanced - often through a series of quite distinct stages.

For the geography teacher who has yet to attempt to use Mysteries we would offer the following suggestions. The application of any new teaching and learning technique implies that the teacher has to engage in a process of professional development; a process which many find difficult given its tendency to make the skilled practitioner feel

like a novice. Often the students will have become used to certain ways of teaching and learning and may demonstrate either passive or active resistance to any new methods. Therefore, in establishing the use of Mysteries within the classroom, we must:

- expect that in the initial stages things will not always go smoothly and that students may resist your attempts to make them work in more challenging ways;
- talk to other teachers (who may not be geographers) within, or beyond, the school environment who are attempting similar things;
- support others who attempt to use similar materials for the first time. There is much to be learnt from watching and working with colleagues going through the same stages of professional development you went through when you first adopted the techniques; and
- gain the support of others; be they senior managers, other teachers, researchers, subject advisors or university tutors.

There are also implications for classroom practice during the use of Mysteries. We would expect that lessons would reveal a number of needs. These may include, for example:

- adjusting our approach to the 'delivery' of subject knowledge. The geographical themes and content to be covered may be the same, but the routes and processes to achieve this coverage are very different;
- the creation of an element of uncertainty about the geographical content, or concepts, being studied. Students must be given the responsibility to question and therefore clarify what they know and understand; and
- the development of a range of techniques and skills to create, introduce, manage and debrief the Mysteries used. The management of group work, the encouragement of discussion and the skills of effective debriefing are essential.

We believe that Mysteries have major potential for practitioner research as they invoke complex processes which can be captured directly, in the case of language, and indirectly (through observation, the movement of the data items and stimulated recall) in the case of thought. Such a research base can help to overcome the difficulties of implementation as there is little doubt that many teachers find the effective use of Mysteries an uphill task (Leat, 1999). To get you started we offer the Mysteries published by Northumberland County Council (1997); in Leat (1998) and on pages 12-1-5. Use them to gain experience of the application of Mysteries in the geography classroom. Adapt and alter them to suit your own curricular needs, and use them to triangulate your observations with ours and those of colleagues.

Educational research is often criticised because of the lack of studies which seek to ascertain whether findings are valid and reliable in other contexts. While we believe the research reported here makes a contribution to the field of work developed by the Thinking Through Geography group, many questions remain either partly or wholly unanswered. So we want to discover whether other teachers/researchers find evidence of similar stages of learning development occurring when they use Mysteries. We would welcome feedback on whether the context in which Mysteries are taught has an influence

upon this. There are also a variety of avenues along which this research could now progress. We suggest four, each with a variety of questions which could be considered in that area.

Research area 1: Research into the influence of students on the outcomes of Mysteries

- What difference does it make if the students have already worked with Mysteries?
- Does student age have a significant impact on the ways in which Mysteries are solved or the solutions they offer?
- How do mixed ability groups operate in comparison to more homogeneous ability groups?
- Do male and female groups differ in the ways in which they tackle Mysteries?

Research area 2: Research into the use and development of student language during the solving of Mysteries

- How do we analyse the discourse of students who are engaged in Mysteries?
- What are the prospects of using audio or video recordings of students at work to understand how their language and thinking develop?
- Is there evidence of progression in the ways in which students talk when solving a series of Mysteries?
- Is the reworking of information accompanied by a different form of student talk?

Research area 3: Research into the most effective forms of teacher intervention to support students in solving Mysteries

- When is the most suitable time to support students, and in what way?
- Can teacher intervention detract from, rather than enhance, the development of students' thinking through geography?
- Does peer support offer a different, and sometimes more effective, form of guidance to students compared to that provided by the teacher?

Research area 4: Research into student learning

- What do students really learn by doing Mysteries?
- What can students tell us about the whole process of their learning development?
- Does student thinking progress through a series of stages reflected by the ways in which they handle the information provided?

A strong reason for tackling such research questions is that they have an unusually high return in terms of professional development, because we begin to see school, lessons, teaching and many students in a completely different light.

Bibliography

Ausubel, D. (1967) *Learning Theory and Classroom Practice*. Toronto: Ontario Institute for Studies in Education.

Biggs, J. and Collis, K. (1982) *Evaluating the Quality of Learning: The structure of learning outcomes*. New York: Academic Press.

Black, P. and Wiliam, D. (1998) 'Assessment and classroom learning', *Assessment in Education: Principles, policy and practice* (special issue on assessment and classroom learning), 5, 1, pp. 7-74.

Brown, A. (1978) 'Knowing when, where, and how to remember: a problem of metacognition' in Glaser, R. (ed) *Advances in Instructional Psychology, Book 1*. Hillsdale NJ: Lawrence Erlbaum Associates.

Brown, A.L. and Campione, J.C. (1990) 'Communities of learning and thinking, or a context by any other name' in Kuhn, D. (ed) *Developmental Perspectives on Teaching and Learning Thinking Skills* (Contributions to Human Development series). Basle: Karger.

Brown, A.L., Campione, J.C., Webber, L.S. and McGilly, K. (1992) 'Interactive learning environments: a new look at assessment and instruction' in Gifford, B.R. and O'Connor, M.C. (eds) *Alternative Views of Aptitude, Achievement and Instruction*. Boston MA: Kluwer Academic.

Brown, J., Collins, A. and Duguid, P. (1989) 'Situated cognition and the culture of learning', *Educational Researcher*, 18, pp. 32-42.

Chall, J., Jacobs, V. and Baldwin, L. (1990) *The Reading Crisis: Why poor children fall behind*. Cambridge MA: Harvard University Press.

Cooper, P. and MacIntyre, D. (1995) *Effective Teaching and Learning: Teachers' and pupils' perspectives*. Milton Keynes: Open University Press.

DfEE/QCA (1999) *The National Curriculum Handbook for Secondary Teachers: key stages 3 and 4*. London: DfEE/QCA.

DfEE (2001) *Literacy Across the Curriculum*. (DfEE 0235/2001). London: DfEE.

DfES (2002) *Training Materials for the Foundation Subjects* (DfES 0350/2002). London: DfES.

DfES (2003) *Teaching and Learning in secondary schools: Pilot* (DfES 0345/2003). London: DfES.

Egan, K. (1988) *Teaching as Story Telling: An alternative approach to teaching and curriculum in the elementary school*. London: Routledge.

Feuerstein, R. (1980) *Instrumental Enrichment*. Baltimore MD: University Park Press.

Flavell, J. (1977) *Cognitive Development* (first edition). Englewood Cliffs NJ: Prentice Hall.

Gentner, D. and Stevens, K. (eds) (1986) *Mental Models*. Hillsdale NJ: Lawrence Erlbaum Associates.

Greenhough, P. and Hughes, M. (1998) 'Parents' and Teachers' interventions in children's reading', *British Educational Research Journal*, 24, pp. 383-98.

Halford, G. (1993) *Children's Understanding: The development of mental models*. Hillsdale NJ: Lawrence Erlbaum Associates.

Hatano, G. and Inagaki, K. (1992) 'Desituating cognition through the construction of conceptual knowledge' in Light, P. and Butterworth, G. (eds) *Context and Cognition*. Hemel Hempstead: Harvester Wheatsheaf, pp. 116.

Leat, D. (1997) 'Getting ambiguous', *Educating Able Children*, 1, pp. 17-25.

Leat, D. (ed) (1998) *Thinking Through Geography*. Cambridge: Chris Kington Publishing.

Leat, D. (1999) 'Rolling the stone uphill: teacher development and the implementation of thinking skills programmes', *Oxford Review of Education*, 25, pp. 387-403.

Leat, D. and Chandler, S. (1996) 'Using concept mapping in geography teaching', *Teaching Geography*, 21, 3, pp. 108-12.

Mason, L. (1996) 'An analysis of children's construction of new knowledge through their use of reasoning and arguing in classrooms', *Qualitative Studies in Education*, 3, pp. 411-33.

McPartland, M.F. (1998) 'The use of narrative in geography teaching', *The Curriculum Journal*, 9, pp. 341-55.

Mercer, N. (1992) 'Context and construction of knowledge in the classroom' in Light, P. and Butterworth, G. (eds) *Context and Cognition*. Oxford: Harvester Wheatsheaf.

Moll, L. (ed) (1990) *Vygotsky and Education: Instructional implications and applications of socio-historical psychology*. Cambridge: Cambridge University Press.

Nichols, A. with Kinninment, D. (2001) *More Thinking Through Geography*. Cambridge: Chris Kington Publishing.

Nisbet, J. and Shucksmith, J. (1986) *The Seventh Sense, Reflections on Learning to Learn*. Edinburgh: Scottish Council for Research in Education.

Northumberland County Council (1997) *Northumberland 'Thinking Skills' in the Humanities Project*. Morpeth: Northumberland CC.

Perkins, D. and Salomon, G. (1988) 'Teaching for transfer', *Educational Leadership*, 46, pp. 22-32.

Pontecorvo, C. (1990) 'Social context, semiotic mediation, and forms of discourse in constructing knowledge at school' in Mandl, H., De Corte, E., Bennett, S. and Friedrich, H. (eds) *Learning and Instruction, European research in an international context: 2:1 Analysis of complex skills and complex knowledge domains*. Oxford: Pergamon Press, pp. 1-26.

Powney, J. and Watts, P. (1987) *Interviewing in Educational Research*. London: Routledge & Kegan Paul.

SCAA (1996) *Key Stage 3 Optional Tests and Tasks: Geography unit 2*. London: SCAA.

SCAA (1997) *Extended Writing in Key Stage 3 History* (Discussion Paper no. 8). London: SCAA.

Stanford, G. (1990) *Developing Effective Classroom Groups – A practical guide for teachers* (adapted for British edition by Pam Stoate). Bristol: Acora Books.

Vygotsky, L. (1978) 'Mind in society' in Cole, M., John-Steiner, V., Scribner, S. and Souberman, E. (eds) *The Development of Higher Psychological Processes*. Cambridge: Cambridge University Press.

Wertsch, J.V. (ed) (1985) *Culture, Communication and Cognition: Vygotskyan perspectives*. New York: Cambridge University Press.

White, S.H. (1989) 'Foreword' to Newman, D., Griffin, P. and Cole, M. (eds) *The Construction Zone*. Cambridge: Cambridge University Press.

Wiliam, D. (1992) 'Some technical issues in assessment: a user's guide', *British Journal for Curriculum and Assessment*, 2, pp. 11-20.

Wood, D., Bruner, J.S. and Ross, G. (1976) 'The role of tutoring in problem solving', *Journal of Child Psychology and Psychiatry*, 17, pp. 89-100.

Wood, D. and Wood, H. (1996) 'Vygotsky, tutoring and learning', *Oxford Review of Education*, 22, pp. 5-16.

Wray, D. and Lewis, M. (1997) *Extending Literacy*. London: Routledge.